Extreme Directions

ALSO BY ALICE JONES

Anatomy
Isthmus
The Knot

Extreme Directions

The 54 Moves of Tai Chi Sword

Alice Jones

OMNIDAWN
RICHMOND, CALIFORNIA
2002

Acknowledgements

I'm grateful to Alan Goldfarb, Ed Smallfield and Rusty Morrison
for their comments on the manuscript.

Book cover and interior design by Philip Krayna Design, Berkeley, California
www.pkdesign.net

Cover illustration: *Embroidered column hanging, Late Ming Dynasty, China*

Library of Congress Cataloging-in-Publication Data

Jones, Alice.
Extreme directions : the 54 moves of tai chi sword / Alice Jones.
    p. cm.
ISBN 1-890650-11-0 (alk. paper)
1. Tai chi—Poetry. I. Title.
PS3560.O4557 E96 2002
811'.54—dc21

                    2001007568

MNIDAWN®

Published by Omnidawn Publishing
Richmond, California
www.omnidawn.com
(800) 792-4957

ISBN: 1-890650-11-0 (paper)
9 8 7 6 5 4 3 2 1

Printed in the United States on archival, acid-free recycled paper.

*This sequence evolved from my observation of
the daily practice of Tai Chi Sword. I wanted the poems
to evoke the movements' fluidity, like Chinese brush
stroke paintings—one quick gesture. Each poem title is
the name of one of the fifty four movements with
translation from the Chinese provided by Wong Yoo-Chong.
Tai Chi literally means the outer-most limits,
great polarities, hence—extreme directions.*

太極劍五十四式

起
式

Beginning form

Wide globe
　　round arms
　　　　want latitude

　　　　improbable regions
　　　　　　east's sword dance

　　you
untranslatable
　　　into me

we're a mouth

　　　　　kiss the diameter
　　make time　　go long

三
環
盦
月

Three rings cover the moon

Where is
    our cloud-sphere
the you/me thing

            penumbra
                    possibility

time and its solutions
        weather

            are we still going

                    outside?

大
魁
星　*Big Dipper*

Silly fool, lost boy
　　　the bucket fell over
　　　　　all by itself

　　star-poured
　　　　another story gone

燕子抄水 *Swallow splashes water*

Ladle skims surface

mirror
              a little zoom

       concentric ripples

                        gone

左右攔掃

Block, sweep left and right

Are you Zorro in the morning
under the covers
unmasked?

小
魁
星 *Little dipper*

Somebody's always got the upper hand

star-spilt
milk-pour

reach in, coming under

燕子入巢 *Swallow enters nest*

Whose baby are you?
　　mine is gone wandering
　　　　crying until
　　the circle closes

虎
抱
頭 *Tiger cradles head*

Who growls louder
you or the freeway?   hold on
there's a curve coming
furry edged swerve
tangent, arc

departure's morning

靈
貓
捕
鼠

Astute cat catches mice

Owlish ear-hairs
eyebrows twitch
rattle in her throat
and the rump does
its preparatory wiggle
poor prey
aimed at,

toy

蜻
蜓
點
水

Dragonfly skims water

Your hand's slow gradient
　　　along the horizon

　　　of my half-asleep flank

黃
蜂
入
洞

Yellow-jacket enters cave

You're the shape of
　　what you long for—
　　　　　　　empty bowl

左
旋
風 *Left whirlwind*

The past pulls on us
          as if wanting to be
some kind of oasis

          as if we could rest there
          sand waving like ocean
          eating dates
                    sweet ooze
          gazing on time's mirage

小魁星 *Little dipper*

Thirsty?

drink

the hours' long tongue

右
旋
風   *Right whirlwind*

The future's magnet
    makes the hairs go gray
        makes us choose
denial, or refusing that

        the old skin softens
    equator's fullness
      dearer
        than we knew

等魚式 *Waiting for fish*

I know they're down there
　　　　　wind-riffled surface

　　still pool

　　only one breath

撥
草
尋
蛇

Parting grass to find snakes

We wanted up and they went down
wandering into the core

they always wanted
to go there, it's the journey
you never pretended to take

inward, fruitful
and winding

懷
中
抱
月 *Cradle the moon on belly*

Held in one circle, woven basket
tender orange fruits
germinate

unpronounced ones
sweeter than you imagined

indefensible rind
we like peeling
we like thinking of eating

宿
鳥
投
林

Resident birds descend upon forest

Whoosh   no

soundless
a green leafy rocking

water
without wet

烏龍擺尾 *Black dragon swishes tail*

Time catches up
and he's bruising

breath's heat
skin's scaling

so transient
watched flame

風
卷
荷
葉

Wind curls up lotus leaf

Frog leap

    green lapped
        golden carp

fold your tongue backwards

    there's more color
        the hidden water-side

獅子搖頭 *Lion shakes head*

We gather whatever
finds us

treed sleep
any liquid

gazelles
stronger than they look
sudden

the nightfall around here

虎
抱
頭 *Tiger cradles head*

If no one holds on to the center
　　　if there are no magnetic poles

oh dear, is every ship a lost one?

野
馬
跳   *Wild horse leaps creek*
澗

Fly globe-wise and somebody
won't catch you, skyborn
going forth
lips reaching
the ears curved pathways
have you heard this before?

a fairy tale
is always retold

勒
馬
式 *Rein horse*

OK, don't fly
            stay in the realm
    of the probable

        here
            we can pay the bills

    sorry again

指
南
針   *South-pointing needle*

Directionality—
　　do we have preferences?
　When east meets west
　　　under the covers
　　　　if north
　gets inside of south
　　　if the phoenix is on top
　if the globe is still turning
　　　and meanwhile the galactic periphery
is moving outwards
　　　　　　at so and so per hour
　　　　are you dancing?
　　we're already home

迎
風
拂
塵

Sweep dust with the wind

Brushed   the long tangles
                    black boats go west
            east is beyond us
                        lost broom straw
        left behind

順
水
推
舟

Push boat downstream

Northness, no one's looking down
on us

effortful

the density of rivers

everyone's feet
glued to the same globe

流星趕月

Meteor chases the moon

Pursued and provoking
　　did you get what you want?

　　no, it's always only try
　　but I've got you
　　　　held in the field
　　　　　　of my reaching eye

天馬飛跑

Skyhorse flies, gallops

What's nice about the mythic is
      the only direction is the improbable
and inside
     fleet-footed
        mane tossing

     we get quite certain

挑
帘
式   *Lift a shade*

He tried to raise her
                from the dead land
        always believing one's own song
            more powerful than time

                        mirror says
            the world is still flat

                hauling with your own old arms
        learn the same thing again

                    the same ungiving marble
                            the same fall

車
輪
劍 *Cartwheel sword*

When you spin yourself
        you've no idea what will get cut
        your own pink skin
        or time's honed edge
upside-down, you don't always know
                who cuts you

燕
子
啣
坭 *Swallow mouths mud*

It's this home-building
      that makes us want to hold on
earthquakes, typhoon
who has time for sculpture
    so much to lose
        you cling
      to each drop of mud you can

大
鵬
單
展
翅

Great roc unfurls single wing

Who could name you?
　　　the spread of time
　　　　　　one-winged
can't touch
　　　　if you close
　　　your eyes
　　　　　　　　(you wish)
　　　black feathers
　　　　　　frightening in their gleam

海底撈月

Scooping up moon from sea bottom

I want you like jewels
    I want you like what I can't reach
        the lost that's forever dreamed of
        the dream that's hidden and held

    you're the sea things get inside of
        the north
      my compass can find

懷
中
抱
月

Cradle the moon on belly

Hold a globe
　　inside a globe
　　　　molten, magma
　　certain seasons
　　　　the pole's magnetic auroras
　　　light folds inside its own sheets

夜
叉
探   *Night spirit explores ocean*
海

        Wading into dark
immersed

           poured
                by what you can't see
      a fluid you were birthed into

          floating all you'd want to find
            eroding all you'd want to hold
        home for whoever
              needs no air

犀
牛
望
月

Rhinoceros gazes at moon

Large and unwieldy
　　ancient and scaled
　　horn designates up
　　　　points with wild longing
　　neighs towards what
　　　　like himself
　　　　　　can't be known

射雁式 *Shoot flying geese*

Wing-claps precede them
  a low sound
        homing for water

      the long flight
        a map encoded
            let's stop here

    one night

青
龍
探
爪

Green dragon searches with claws

The mountain they call Green Dragon
curled and sleeps on its side
no smoke emerging

distant gong

one stretched hand
admired
aimed

鳳
凰
雙
展
翅

Phoenix spreads both wings

Flight

we longed for it like water
          like sails
    ground   undeserved in its missing

        air undeserved in its breadth

左右挎攔 *Stride, block left and right*

Two sides
　　to every question

　　　our reaching, kneading
　　　　　sphere beyond oneself

　　　　longitude
　　grainy
　　　　　the chewiness
　　　　　　of longing

射
雁
式   *Shoot flying geese*

Don't envy that sureness—
　　the arrow only points one way

　　landing gear folded up
　　　kept warm
　　　　skating
　　　　　　touching down

　　silvered lake
　　　floating today's
　　　　webbed forms

白猿獻果

White monkey offers up fruit

Hungry ghost   the sole purpose

     a gift

        eyes   tongue   fingers

pleasures   of wanting
   pleasures of bringing

      an offered cup spills over

左右落花

Drop flowers left and right

South   Spring
            some for you
        some for me

        the season's offerings
            thin-veined

grow up through clay
    you never thought
            those scents would continue
        arriving each day

玉
女
穿
梳

Jade maiden shuttling comb

Hair in its blackness
loom
in its readiness
interweaving
east and west
warped woof
twined roof of dry twigs
the furze layer on top

rain-feeding
makes winter go green

白
虎
攬
尾

White tiger curls tail

All proud of possession
    furled and held stately
you'll see the tail when I'm hunting
      purring in snowfall
admiring the phoebe's hops
a mouthful still moving
    brisk   purposeful
    each whisker's tripped twitch

虎抱頭 *Tiger cradles head*

Migraines too? the packed growl
undigested bird wings
knit one creature
inside another
feathers are to fur
as north to south

rocking

the arms' warm bowl

鯉
魚
跳
龍
門

Carp leaps dragon gate

We've gone all directions
        nameless and sprouting
things and their belongings beyond us
            out in the next place
    scales gill frills   the gold back

        look over one shoulder

            absent
                    with grace

烏
龍
紋
柱

Black dragon wraps around column

The hegemony of dragons
how they like their possessions
black smoke
wreath-worn
a vanished power
holds up the roof

仙人指路 *An immortal points the way*

Probably not

each circle
one center

without arms   could go anywhere
follow
if you can

懷
中
抱
月

Cradle the moon on belly

Throw out the baby-water

       when inside turns to out
       when gibbous turns to crescent
          when the near black sphere
              fills in its emptiness

     who is it   who's fed now?

風
掃
梅
花

Wind sweeps plum flowers

Why was the broom considered holy?
in several directions
a workable scatter

wasn't it snow?

指南針 *South-pointing needle*

All indications are

raise the shade and look
the emboldened warrior
finds the black-haired maiden

the four beauties of direction
found here at the center

we didn't find the tropics
but they ringed us

exhaling plant air
bloom here

持劍歸原

Sword back to origin

Globe circled   waist rounding
      time   having his way
                with us again

    side-slip
      so certain
        of nothing
          but the circle

ALICE JONES'S books, *The Knot,* which won the Beatrice Hawley Award, and *Isthmus,* recipient of the Jane Kenyon Chapbook Award, are both published by  Alice James Books. *Anatomy* was published by Bullnettle Press. She has been awarded fellowships by the Bread Loaf Writers Conference and the National Endowment for the Arts. A manuscript of prose poems won the Robert H. Winner Award from the Poetry Society of America in 2001. Poems have appeared in *Ploughshares, Volt, Colorado Review, Poetry, The Harvard Review, Chelsea, Denver Quarterly,* and *Best American Poetry of 1994.* She is a co-editor of Apogee Press.